WARSHIPS IN ACTION TODAY

E.L.Cornwell

LONDON

IAN ALLAN LTD

Contents

First published 1980

ISBN 0 7110 1024 2

© Ian Allan Ltd 1980

Published by Ian Allan Ltd, Shepperton, Surrey, and printed by Ian Allan Printing Ltd at their works at Coombelands in Runnymede, England.

Introduction

During the past decade or so advances in technology have brought about fundamental changes in naval strategy. The changes have followed each other at regular intervals, sometimes with a rapidity that has rendered costly new equipment obsolescent, even obsolete, before it has properly been worked up to full operational efficiency.

We have seen the designation 'capital ship' pass from the centuries-long holder — the big-gunned battleship — to the aircraft carrier with its longer reach, for a brief period during and after World War II, and now to the nuclear-powered ballistic missile-armed submarine, where it seems likely to rest for a long time to come. Unlike its two predecessors, today's capital ship is not photogenic and it figures in only a few pictures in this book. But with its high submerged speed, freedom from the need to surface frequently, ability to lurk virtually undetectable in the ocean depths and a hitting power in one small vessel greater than all the armaments of the last war put together it is certainly a most potent weapon and a worthy capital ship.

Just as the big guns and their carrying vessels have been completely outclassed by the hydrogen bomb warhead and nuclear propulsion, so smaller supporting weapons and the fleet escorts that deploy them have been fundamentally changed by the guided missile and the electronics needed for their aiming and control. As these have become more complex and specialised the form and size of ships to carry them have had to change. Overall the trend is away from the multi-capability or general-purpose ship towards vessels, usually smaller than those they replace, designed and equipped for a specialised role, with a particular emphasis on countering the threat of the ballistic missile-armed submarine.

In fact, the anti-submarine theme runs right through the modern navy's inventory, from the new-style aircraft carrier right down to light escorts, and only the very smallest warships are built today without the ability to operate helicopters for anti-submarine work. Probably the most efficient defence against the missile submarine is, ironically enough, the hunter/killer submarine which, to be effective, must match its quarry in speed, operating depth, range and ability to avoid detection and must itself therefore have nuclear propulsion. Only the American, Russian and British navies have nuclear-powered hunter/killer submarines.

There is rather wider distribution among world navies of what is in effect a fairly new and still developing form of ship — the anti-submarine cruiser. The breed started with the fairly drastic conversion of cruiser- and destroyer-size ships so that they could house and operate several heavy anti-submarine helicopters; it has included various older conventional aircraft carriers adapted to fill a specialised anti-submarine role, and has been consolidated in new classes of aircraft carrier or sea control ship represented by the Russian *Kiev* and British *Invincible* designs. The evolution of the specialist helicopter-V/STOL carrier is traced through the pictures in this book.

Most widely used defence against the submarine is the shipborne helicopter and virtually all warships of corvette size and above entering service today have accommodation for one, and many new frigates and destroyers can operate two. The helicopter deck and accommodation, the various types of guided missile that largely replace the traditional gun, the rather exotic aerial and director arrays and radomes, and new-style uptakes to go with gas turbine engines have all contributed to a fresh variety and individuality in the appearance of ships, and they are all widely represented in the pictures in this book.

The recent quickened pace of change has led to massive increases in the real costs of maintaining naval forces at traditional levels. In all countries except those with totalitarian economies the trend has been towards spending more and more on social welfare and individual indulgence and a dwindling proportion on defence. While, in the abstract, that might be a desirable trend if it was universally applied, the inevitable result has been a relative weakening of the military capabilities of the Western democracies to the point where collectively, at least in numbers of men and weapons, they have been or are rapidly being overtaken by the totalitarian states — chiefly Soviet Russia.

With huge land frontiers to guard, great Soviet strength in land and defensive air forces could be viewed without fear or suspicion of aggressive intent, but the rapid advancement of the Soviet naval arm towards a position of numerical superiority is one to be viewed quite differently. It is obvious that the Soviet Union has small need of overseas supplies compared with the complete dependence of most of the Western democracies on seaborne traffic — in peace or war. Yet Soviet naval strength is already well in excess of what can be deemed reasonable for defence and is still being expanded. So the question must be asked: Why does Russia need superiority in naval forces if not for conquest, or the threat of aggression to achieve political ends inimical to Western interests?

As far as it is possible to judge in the traditional secrecy surrounding Soviet defence spending, with the observable output of armaments, and particularly of warships and aircraft, there has clearly been a substantial annual increase throughout the 1970s. Current Soviet military spending is reliably estimated to be well over 10 per cent of the gross national product and to be rising, which compares with between five and six per cent by the United States, five per cent by the United Kingdom and substantially less by other Western democracies (although France has recently announced a small increase to between three-and-a-half and four per cent).

All this means that the numerical superiority of Russian naval forces is likely to increase rather than diminish, and their potential effectiveness is increased by recent political shifts that have afforded them havens in most of the possible areas of any future conflict. In such circumstances, if aggression is to be discouraged, certain actions by the democracies are essential. Chief among them is the need for individual nations to show unequivocally the will and the intention to resist any threat of aggression. A second requirement is for the NATO allies to continue to show that they can and they will react together and quickly. A third is that numerical inferiority must be more than offset by technical superiority in equipment and in its manner of deployment.

Demonstration of the first of these desiderata is not always so evident as to provide much deterrent effect. Would-be aggressors must have taken great comfort from the frequent cuts in defence spending by the Western democracies in recent years, and from the reluctance of some states to contribute anything more than lip service to the provision of a common front against what appears to be a sustained communist bid for world hegemony. Even so, there remains a considerable will by many governments to make the sacrifices necessary to maintain effective naval forces, as this book illustrates in nearly 200 pictures of the warships of many nationalities.

On the second consideration also, the NATO Alliance has its disappointing and its heartening aspects, with some of its constituents contributing up to the point almost of national sacrifice and others appearing less than wholehearted in their support. Here again, this book provides grounds for confidence in the numbers of warships of different nationalities pictured working together. Further encouragement can perhaps be derived from the recent indication that France is likely at last to emerge from its (to the rest of the world at least) futile nationalistic isolation, a move which would greatly strengthen the Western naval forces charged with maintaining a balance in the deteriorating Mediterranean theatre, and from the possibility that the British Navy is again to station ships in the Indian Ocean.

On the third requirement, superiority of equipment and the way it is used – in effect, the men and the methods – probably only a war could give a positive answer. What is known is that during the last few years there has been a complete revolution in surveillance, detection and identification equipment, in the integration and transmission of information so gathered and in the automatic direction and actuation of the various weapon systems. In those high-technology areas, if not in numbers of weapons and the magnitude of their blasts, the West has so far always maintained a significant lead.

In selecting the pictures for this book no attempt has been made to include ships of every nationality nor even of every class, and in some cases the quality of the photograph rather than its subject has influenced the choice. Nor is every detail catalogued in uniform style for every ship pictured; various catalogues exist that already provide that service. The captions generally give enough infor-mation to show each subject's nationality, class, capabilities and any special features. The overall objective has been to produce an attractive and interesting picture book that gives a reasonably balanced coverage of the warships in service around the world in the 1970s.

The assembly of such a mass of pictures of warships of many types and nationalities in an intelligible way was rather more of a problem than it would have been a few years ago, when there was a fairly clear division into well-defined classes. Today, except for submarines, there is no such distinction and the arrangement of the material into five sections is the author's own and quite arbitrary, But it was convenient and seemed logical to group all ships designed or adapted to operate four or more heavy helicopters, except assault and auxiliary ships, with aircraft carriers, and all fighting ships with a standard displacement of about 1,000 tons or over with the principal surface warships. The others fell naturally into chapters covering submarines, assault and small patrol craft, and auxiliaries.

Tonnages given in the captions are mainly of standard displacement, in most cases rounded up or down to the nearest 50 tons, except for cargo vessels where the customary grt (gross registered tons) is used. Displacement figures preceded by the letter c (circa) indicate an approximation because published data was not immediately available or conflicted and figures followed by dl (deep load) are used where only that information was known or reliable. Tonnages given for submarines generally are for submerged displacement.

Aircraft Carriers

Three pictures illustrating international cooperation in naval exercises involving aircraft carriers:

Below: The British anti-submarine/commando carrier *Hermes* (R12, 28,500 tons) deploying Sea Vixen and Gannet aircraft before conversion to her present role, providing stores and fuel to the Indian light cruiser *Mysore* ex-HMS *Nigeria* (C60, 8,700 tons)./*British Aerospace*

Right : The US carrier *America* (CV66, 60,200 tons), one of four Kitty Hawk ships, heading the British County class guided-missile destroyer *Antrim* (D18, 5,450 tons) and frigates *Andromeda* (F57), *Naiad* (F39), *Bacchante* (F69), *Charybdis* (F75) and *Yarmouth* (F101), in the 1976 NATO exercise Display Determination, which involved about 60 ships of six nationalities./*MoD*

Below right: In the same NATO exercise, the British carrier *Ark Royal* (R09, 43,000 tons) leading the American guided-missile cruiser *Albany* (CG10 ex-CA123, 13,900 tons) and two columns of US escort ships./ *HMS Ark Royal*

Left: Mightiest warship ever built (and perhaps ever likely to be built), USS *Dwight D. Eisenhower* (CVN69, 78,000 tons), completed in 1976 as second of a class of three nuclear-powered aircraft carriers; *Nimitz* (CVN68) was first of the three completed a year earlier and the third, *Carl Vinson* (CVN70), is due for completion in 1981. The class deploys 90 aircraft of seven or eight types, including the F-14 Tomcat swing-wing 'air superiority' fighter, the A-6E Intruder low-level bomber, the E-2C Hawkeye airborne early warning aircraft and various reconnaissance, electronic countermeasures, airborne refueller, fighter control and anti-submarine types./*US Navy*

Above: First of the Nimitz class, *Nimitz* herself, which, apart from pennant number, is distinguishable from the *Eisenhower* in having two forward deck-edge horns and a third on the angled deck compared with a single horn on the later ship. /*Inter-Air Press*

Right: A Corsair ground-attack aircraft being prepared for take-off as others are catapulted from the *Nimitz* when she was stationed with the Sixth Fleet in the Mediterranean in 1978. The A-7E Corsair II by LTV Aerospace won a 1963 design contest for a lightweight attack aircraft. It is powered by a Rolls-Royce Spey-derived Allison turbofan and is armed with a 20mm multi-barrel cannon and up to about 15,000lb of a variety of missiles, bombs or gun packs./*Inter-Air Press*

10

Above left: The US Navy's first nuclear-powered carrier was the *Enterprise* (CVN65, 75,500 tons), here seen in the Pacific in 1978 during exercise Rimpac. The *Enterprise* was completed in 1961 as a slightly enlarged Kitty Hawk-class ship and was intended to be one of a pair; in the event, because of the cost, the second, *John F. Kennedy* (CV67), was completed as one of the standard conventionally powered Kitty Hawks./*US Navy*

Left: Preparing a Tomcat fighter for launching from the starboard catapult of USS *Enterprise* as one has just left the port catapult. The Grumman F-14A Tomcat is a two-seat twin-engined fighter with a top speed approaching Mach 2.5; armament includes a multi-barrel gun, Sparrow or Phoenix air-to-air missiles, and Sidewinder missiles in place of external fuel tanks./*US Navy*

Above: As escorts for its first nuclear-powered carrier the United States Navy introduced also the nuclear-powered cruiser *Long Beach* (CGN9, 14,200 tons) and frigate *Bainbridge* (DLGN25, 7,600 tons) to form a battle group with unprecedented range and freedom from frequent refuelling. The practice has been continued and here the *Eisenhower* is seen with CGN36 *California*, CGN37 *South Carolina* and CGN38 *Virginia* exercising as nuclear task force CTF21./*US Navy*

Right: One of the *Eisenhower*'s Tomcats on the port lift, which, as on many US carriers, is outside the hull. There are three more outside elevators on the starboard side, two ahead of the island and one aft abreast of the port unit./*Ambrose Greenway*

Left: An advantage of nuclear propulsion is that no uptakes are necessary, permitting a smaller and neater island, as this picture of *Nimitz* taken at the Queen's Jubilee Review at Spithead in 1978 shows, and freedom from uptake air pollution. /*Ambrose Greenway*

Scenes during flying operations aboard USS *Dwight D. Eisenhower* with the Sixth Fleet in the Mediterranean in 1979:

Below: Landing signals officers guiding aircraft in from the LSO platform; *Right:* a Tomcat on landing approach, hook extended, viewed between the island superstructure and other Tomcats and a Hawkeye on deck; and, *Below right,* a Corsair just touching down under watchful eyes in primary flight control /*All: Ambrose Greenway*

Above: As well as the three nuclear-powered multi-role attack carriers and a fourth nearing completion, the US Navy has four of the big conventionally powered Kitty Hawks that practically match the nuclear units in all but fuel range. Here one of the four, *John F. Kennedy* (CV67, 61,000 tons), with escorting Leahy-class missile frigate *Dale* (CG19, 5,700 tons), takes stores from supply ship USS *Sylvania* (AFS21) during a 1978 exercise in the Mediterranean./*US Navy*

Above right: Another picture of the *John F. Kennedy* with Vought Crusader, North American Rockwell Vigilante, Lockheed Viking, Grumman Intruder and Grumman Hawkeye aircraft ranged ('spotted') on deck./*Peter Kilduff*

Right: Haphazard as it might sometimes appear, movement of aircraft to and from the lifts and their positioning on deck call for detailed planning and tight control. Here, aboard class leader *Kitty Hawk* (CV63), crewmen in the deck-control and launch operations room move pieces to represent flightdeck activity and thus ensure smooth flow. The board pattern is duplicated in the hangars./*US Navy*

Left: USS *Midway* (CV41, 51,000 tons) preparing to recover one of her McDonnell Douglas F-4 Phantoms. The *Midway* is a survivor of a class of three (originally planned as six) World War II designed fleet or attack carriers. She was completed in 1945, just too late to see war service (and late enough to have worked in the three British developments of angled deck, steam catapult and mirror landing system) and was the first American design to incorporate a really strong flightdeck. The F-4 Phantom is a Mach 2-plus fighter or fighter/bomber designed for the USN in the 1950s which can carry up to 16,000lb of armaments or stores and has been sold in quantity to about 10 navies and air forces./*US Navy*

Above: A Grumman E-2 Hawkeye about to touch down on USS *Saratoga* (CV60, 59,800 tons), one of four Forrestal class ships completed between 1955 and 1959. The class established the general arrangement of modern American attack carriers and initiated the replacement of conventional ships' weapons by missiles. The Hawkeye is a twin-turboprop carrier-borne early warning and fighter control aircraft operated by a crew of five. It carries no armament but a mass of advanced electronics served by the huge rotating radome producing data which are integrated automatically with those of all other units of a naval task force./*US Navy*

Right: USS *Franklin D. Roosevelt* (CV42), another of the Midways and now paid off, was used for the trials of the British S/VTOL Harrier as a close-support fighter aboard a fleet carrier. The US Marine Corps normally deploys its Harriers, of which it bought over a hundred and is seeking to acquire more of an advanced version, for strike and reconnaissance duties on escort carriers and with commando units. The *Roosevelt* had the distinction of accepting the USN's first planned landing by a jet – a McDonnell FD Phantom (not an F-4 Phantom II) in July 1946 – though there had been an inadvertent jet landing on USS *Wake Island* by a Ryan Fireball in November 1945, preceding the successful HMS *Ocean*/DH Vampire trials by a month./*US Navy*

Left & below: Two pictures showing other Marine Corps operations with Harriers, aboard USS *Guam* (LPH9, 17,000 tons), during evaluation of the sea control ship concept. *Guam* was originally one of the seven Iwo Jima class amphibious assault ships designed to operate up to about 30 helicopters. As an interim sea control ship she carried about eight anti-submarine helicopters and six Harriers to provide fast fighter response while acting as escort for convoys, underway replenishment, small assault forces and so on.
/Both: British Aerospace Kingston

Right: The Soviet Union, after showing little or no interest in naval aviation for many years, in the 1970s suddenly entered the field with a class of three quite large aircraft carriers, the Kuril class of about 40,000 tons displacement. The first, *Kiev*, pictured here, was completed in 1975 and *Minsk* followed in 1978, with a third still building. There are reports in 1979 of a very large hull, possibly with nuclear propulsion and suitable for an aircraft carrier, under construction in Russia; if confirmed, it could initiate renewed activity on big attack carriers which even the Americans have abandoned on the grounds of colossal cost and supposed vulnerability. This picture of *Kiev* shows the angled flightdeck, which is not equipped to take normal fixed-wing aircraft, with Ka-25 Hormone helicopters and two of the Yak-36 Forger VTOL fighter/reconnaissance aircraft. It is estimated that about 30 to 40 mixed Forgers and helicopters can be carried./*MoD (Navy)*

Above & left: Two pictures taken from a Royal Air Force Nimrod in January 1970 of the Russian helicopter carrier *Moskva*, after the ship had entered the Atlantic for the first time. *Moskva* is one of two 15,000ton ships of basically heavy cruiser design forward and aircraft carrier aft, designed to operate about 20 anti-submarine helicopters and/or VTOL fixed-wing aircraft. The ship is very heavily armed with missiles, rockets and automatic guns. It has a massive midships bridge structure with a sheer after end that must create extremely turbulent conditions on the flightdeck and virtually exclude the deployment of even VTOL fixed-wing aircraft, although ship-borne trials of the Yakovlev Freehand, experimental predecessor of the Forger, were carried out on the Moskvas. */Both: MoD (Navy) via A. J. Watts*

Above right: Another view of the Russian carrier *Kiev*, photographed north of the Hebrides in December 1977 and, *Right*, a fine view of her sister *Minsk* showing a foredeck stacked with assorted weaponry taken in the Mediterranean south of Crete in February 1979. Both pictures were taken from RAF Nimrod aircraft./*MoD*

Above left & left: Like other continental European powers, France had little experience with aircraft carriers until after World War II. Then, after gaining experience with two ex-Royal Navy and two ex-US Navy carriers, and after several false starts, the first French-built carrier, *Clemenceau* (R98, 22,000 tons), was completed in 1961, to be followed two years later by a second of the same class, *Foch* (R99), pictured here. The ships are powered for a speed of 32kts and normally carry up to about 40 mixed fighters, fighter/bombers and anti-submarine fixed-wing aircraft and helicopters./*Michael Lennon*

Above & right: Two pictures of the French helicopter cruiser *Jeanne d'Arc* (R97, 10,000 tons), leaving Brest in 1967 soon after commissioning and during landing and take-off trials of the Hawker Siddeley Harrier 'jump jet'. The *Jeanne d'Arc*, designed and built as a specialised training ship in the early 1960s, was temporarily given the name *La Résolue* until the paying off of her training ship predecessor of the same name./*ECP Armées via A. J. Watts; British Aerospace Kingston*

Above left: Although the Royal Navy has paid off its last conventional aircraft carrier several other of the world's navies retain British-built carriers in active service. The one pictured here is the Brazilian Navy's *Minas Gerais* (All, 15,900 ton, ex-HMS *Vengeance* of the Majestic (Colossus) class, which was completed early in 1945 and reached the Far East just in time to see the end of the Japanese war. Others of the same class are the Argentine Navy's *25 de Mayo*, the Indian Navy's *Vikrant* and the Royal Australian Navy's *Melbourne*, pictured on page 26. Brazil bought the *Minas Gerais* in 1956 and she was remodelled by a Dutch yard with angled deck, steam catapult and new superstructure before joining the Brazilian fleet in 1961. She is now equipped primarily as an anti-submarine carrier and, as the picture shows, has run trials with the Harrier./*British Aerospace*

Left: A carrier of even earlier vintage is operated by the Spanish Navy in the *Dédalo* (PH01, 11,000 tons) ex-USS *Cabot* (AVT3). Originally one of a class of American cruiser hulls that were

converted and completed as light escort carriers in the early 1940s, the ship was further converted to a specialised anti-submarine carrier and then to an auxiliary aircraft transport before being transferred on loan to Spain in 1967 and finally bought by Spain and named *Dédalo*. The ship is used mainly with anti-submarine helicopters but now operates also British-built Harriers supplied through America at a time when Britain embargoed the sale of arms to Spain. The *Dédalo* seems likely now to complete more than four decades of service because of delay in building her planned successor, to be named *Almirante Carrero*./*Michael Lennon*

Above: A vital role of all carriers today is anti-submarine warfare and of primary importance is the detection and identification of submarines. A main item of detection equipment is the dunking sonar, demonstrated in this picture by a Westland Sea King all-weather helicopter fitted with advanced electronic equipment. /*Westland Aircraft*

Top & above: HMAS *Melbourne* (16,000 tons), flagship of the Royal Australian Navy, was the name ship of the six-strong British Majestic class of light fleet carriers laid down at the end of 1943. Two of the class were allocated to the RAN; the first, HMS *Terrible*, renamed *Sydney*, was completed to the original design and delivered in 1949 and served in the Korean War, but the *Melbourne* was considerably modified to incorporate an angled deck, steam catapults and modern landing aids before eventual commissioning in 1955. Further modernisation was undertaken in 1969, when the new equipment embarked included a squadron of McDonnell A-4G Skyhawks and Wessex helicopters as seen in the lower picture, as well as Grumman S-2 Tracker aircraft./*Both: Inter-Air Press.*

Top right: The Italian Navy started the serious deployment of ship-based anti-submarine helicopters with the two four-helicopter cruisers completed in 1964, *Andrea Doria* (C553) and *Caio Duilio* (C554, 5,000 tons, pictured here). The ships are also armed with surface-to-air missiles, eight 3in automatic guns and six torpedo tubes and have a top speed of 30kts.
/*Italian Navy via A. J. Watt*

Right: As with many pioneering ideas, the early helicopter cruisers were soon outclassed and the Italian Navy followed up with the *Vittorio Veneto* (C550, 7,500 tons), completed in 1969. She is a 32-knot ship designed to operate nine Agusta-Bell helicopters and is armed with a twin launcher for Terrier or Asroc missiles, eight 3in guns and six anti-submarine torpedo tubes./*Italian Navy*

28

Left & above: HMS *Invincible* (R05, 20,000 tons), here pictured on sea trials off the Scottish coast in June 1979, is as new in concept, execution and equipment as anything pioneered by the Royal Navy in its long and illustrious past. The greatest threat to Europe in any future conflict will undoubtedly be from the submarine attempting to block essential supply lines. Planned and built as a 'through-deck cruiser' to soften opposition by the powerful anti-carrier lobby (but often openly referred to as the 'see-through carrier'), the *Invincible,* and her two sisters *Illustrious* and *Ark Royal* now building, are undoubtedly aircraft carriers though officially listed as anti-submarine cruisers. The type has the capacity to operate up to about 20 mixed heavy anti-submarine helicopters and V/STOL Sea Harrier strike/reconnaissance aircraft, the latter's performance rendered considerably more potent by the 'ski-jump' take-off ramp visible in the picture. The new ship is very much more than an aircraft carrier; it is equipped as a command ship to control and coordinate the actions of the many elements of an anti-submarine warfare group at sea in automatic harmony with an overall headquarters ashore. A further claim to novelty of the ship is that it is the biggest warship yet to be powered entirely with gas turbines, having two Rolls-Royce Tynes for economical cruising and four Rolls-Royce Olympuses for very rapid attainment of maximum speed of around 30kts./*MoD (Navy)*

Above left: Old and new concepts of warship-based aircraft are seen together in this picture of the Royal Yacht *Britannia* leading HMS *Eagle* (43,000 tons) and HMS *Blake* (C99, 9,950 tons) in the 1969 Torbay Review. The *Blake* was one of a pair of World War II-designed cruisers (C20 *Tiger* is the other) converted to the new role of missile-armed four-helicopter cruisers in the late 1960s. She is now in reserve. The *Eagle* was disposed of in 1972./*Ambrose Greenway*

Left, above, right: An attractive study of HMS *Bulwark* (R08, 23,300 tons) at anchor off the coast of Malaysia during her second role of commando carrier. Although listed for disposal more than once, *Bulwark* remains in commission as a helicopter carrier and ASW group command ship, pending commissioning of the Invincible-class ships. The other two pictures of *Bulwark* show a typical deck scene, with a Westland Wessex helicopter and Army equipment, and exercising her AA guns against an 'attacking' Canberra./*All: Ambrose Greenway*

Above: HMS *Hermes* (R12, 28,500 tons) was the first of the medium-capacity aircraft carriers completed after the war to be equipped as a helicopter carrier and interim ASW command ship. Like *Bulwark,* she retains the ability to operate in a secondary commando carrier role, in which as well as her own complement of nearly 1,000 men and about 20 helicopters she can provide accommodation for a complete 750-strong commando unit. In an emergency she could take a second commando and a brigade headquarters./*MoD (Navy)*

Submarines

Below: Most likely role of NATO's specialist ASW carriers in any future war is the protection of shipping lanes in the Atlantic and one of the most deadly likely opponents is the Soviet missile-firing submarine (SSGN). One class of SSGN now becoming numerous is the EII Echo nuclear-powered submarine which, unlike the Charlie class boats armed with 30-mile-range missiles, carries cruise missiles of much longer range and hence operates from positons less vulnerable to counter-attack.
/US Navy via A. J. Watts

Bottom: The massive Soviet submarine fleet also includes scores of strategic strike vessels armed with ballistic missiles. Most are now nuclear-powered (SSBN), such as the 16-missile Yankee class, and the older GII Golf diesel-powered boats like the one pictured here are gradually being replaced.
/US Navy via A. J. Watts

Above left: USS *Ohio* (SSBN726), first of the US Navy's Trident missile-firing nuclear-powered submarines and now on sea trials, pictured here under construction in 1978, dwarfing the nuclear-powered attack submarine SSN699 *Jacksonville* during the latter's launching. The Ohio class boats – 13 are so far planned – displace nearly 13,000 tons submerged and are to be armed initially with 24 Trident missiles. The current Trident missile has a multiple-independent-charge warhead (MIRV) and a 4,000-mile range; a later version is expected to range to 6,000 miles./*US Navy*

Left & above: Two more of the American nuclear-powered fast attack submarines, *Memphis* (SSN691) at high speed on the surface during Navy sea trials in 1977 and *Birmingham* (SSN695) surfacing in dramatic fashion during pre-delivery tests in 1979. About a third of the so-far planned 39 boats of this c7,000ton-submerged class have been completed. They are equipped to launch the 60-mile-range anti-ship Harpoon missile while submerged./*Both US Navy*

Right: America's major deterrence weapon for many years has been the fleet of nuclear-powered Polaris/Poseidon missile-armed submarines, one of which, SSBN611 *John Marshall*, is pictured here. It is planned to convert 10 of the Poseidon-armed boats to carry 16 Trident missiles and the first of them, *Francis Scott Key*, is about to be commissioned as this is written. /*US Navy*

Left & bottom left: Half of Great Britain's principal contribution to the West's strategic deterrent is represented here by HMSs *Resolution* and *Repulse,* of the fleet of four nuclear-powered Polaris submarines. Although perhaps appearing insignificant compared with the number of such boats with later and supposedly better (worse?) ballistic missiles deployed by the USA and USSR, in fact just one Polaris submarine, operating virtually undetectably through the successive updatings of its very advanced electronic and sonic equipment, is a weapon no sane government would goad into offensive action. Each of the 7,000ton-plus boats is armed with 16 Polaris missiles with a range of nearly 3,000 miles as well as torpedoes and is manned by two complete crews, has practically unlimited range and does not have to surface for air./*MoD (Navy); Michael Lennon*

Below & bottom: As well as the Polaris fleet, the Royal Navy has two classes of nuclear-powered fleet or attack submarines (SSNs) in commission, illustrated here in the Valiant-class *Churchill* and the later Swiftsure-class *Sceptre.* Both classes can cruise underwater at high speed and remain submerged for very long periods. Displacing about 3,500 tons, they provide comparatively spacious accommodation. A continuing programme of development since the first British SSN, HMS *Dreadnought,* commissioned in 1963 has concentrated on making British boats less detectable while improving their hunter/killer capabilities and at least in the first of those objectives the Royal Navy is widely acknowledged to be very well up with the leaders. All of the proved latest technology is being incorporated in an improved Swiftsure class, the first of which is HMS *Trafalgar* now building./*Both: Michael Lennon*

Left: HMS *Oracle,* one of the diesel-electric Oberon-class patrol submarines which, with earlier Porpoise-class boats, incorporate many of the latest developments of the SSNs and perform similar detection and strike roles though at shorter range. /*Michael Lennon*

Below left: The captain at the periscope in a typical control room of a conventionally powered submarine, claustrophobic conditions now considerably improved in the long-range nuclear-powered boats./*Ambrose Greenway, Popperfoto*

Right: France is the fourth nation to build and operate SSBNs and one of her three ballistic missile-armed boats (SNLE), *Le Terrible,* is pictured; a fourth of the same class is undergoing trials and a fifth is building. They are big craft, of 9,000 tons submerged displacement, each armed with 16 ballistic missiles and 18 torpedoes. A study of a nuclear-powered attack submarine (SNA72) of about 3,000 tons displacement was started in 1976./*ECP Armées via A. J. Watt*

Below: In the meantime, in the attack role the French Navy relies principally on nine boats of the 850ton Daphné class and six 1,900ton Narval class, one of which, *Requin,* is illustrated. Boats of the Daphné class are also operated by the Spanish, Portuguese, Pakistani and South African navies./*Michael Lennon*

Above: The French attack submarine force is being augmented by four new high-performance diesel-electric boats, the first of which to commission, *Agosta,* is illustrated. Spain has also contracted to build two similar with French assistance. *Agosta* displaces 1,725 tons and has a maximum speed of 20kts submerged and is armed with 20 torpedoes for four tubes. */ECP Armées via A. J. Watts*

Left: The Swedish submarine *Sjöhasten* is one of the five-boat Sjöormen class built between 1967 and 1969. It is based on a 167ft Albacore-type high-speed hull with a submerged displacement of 1,400 tons and started the trend towards smaller boats for use in the Baltic Sea. */Royal Swedish Navy via A. J. Watts*

Above right: The *Tonijn* (S805, 1,495/1,825 tons) is the last built (1966) of the Royal Netherlands Navy's four boats of the Dolfijn/Potvis class. It has a unique form of construction comprising three separate hulls in a triangular arrangement inside the casing. It is armed with six torpedo tubes. */Michael Lennon*

Right: The submarine *Piomarta* (ex-USS *Trigger*) (S515, 2,050/ 2,700 tons) is one of two American Tang-class boats completed in 1951/52 and transferred to the Italian Navy in 1973 and 1974. She is powered by three diesels on two shafts to give 15.5-16 knots and armed with six 21in torpedo tubes at bow and two at stern. The domes house PUFFS sonar that gives target range and bearing, even submerged./*Italian Navy*

Major Warships

Below: Ships of six NATO nations that normally operate in the Atlantic make up the Standing Naval Force Atlantic (STANAVFORLANT) Squadron and exercise together regularly in European and North American waters. The squadron is a permanent formation of destroyer-type vessels but individual ships take part on a rotational basis to provide experience of international operation to the greatest number of crews. In this picture the squadron comprises, left to right, *Ambuscade* (F172, 2,000 tons, UK), *Augsburg* (F222, 2,100 tons, W Germany), *Van Galen* (F803, 2,500 tons, Netherlands), *Margaree* (DDE230, 2,250 tons, Canada), *Miller* (FF1091, 3,000 tons, USA) and *Oslo* (F300, 1,450 tons, Norway), and is seen exercising in the Arctic Sea./*NATO*

Right: This picture shows a festive rather than a warlike international gathering, at the Royal Review at Spithead in 1977. Left to right are the Australian carrier *Melbourne* (see page 26), the French missile destroyer *Duquesne* (see page 60) and the Canadian anti-submarine destroyer *Huron* (281, 3,400 tons), with a coastal-type mine countermeasures vessel in the foreground./*Ambrose Greenway*

Below right: A still different kind of joint sortie is pictured here, off Hong Kong, showing a Wessex 5 helicopter landing on missile destroyer HMS *Devonshire* (DO2, 5,450 tons) with Hong Kong Dragon Squadron patrol craft *Yarnton* and *Beachampton* astern./*Hong Kong PR*

Left: Ships of the 1978 STANAVFORLANT squadron in line ahead off Portland. In the picture, from the right, are the Canadian destroyer *Huron,* the Norwegian frigate *Trondheim* (F302, 1,450 tons), the Dutch (Leander) frigate *Tjerk Hiddes* (F804, 2,500 tons) and the West German missile destroyer *Schleswig-Holstein* (D182, 3,400 tons). Out of sight leading the column are the American anti-submarine frigate *Pharris* (FF1094, 3,000 tons) and the British Leander frigate *Phoebe* (F42, 2,450 tons)./*Ambrose Greenway*

Top & above: Two pictures taken during the same 1978 STANAVFORLANT exercises showing, the *Schleswig-Holstein* and the *Tjerk Hiddes* and, the *Pharris* being refuelled from the British fleet tanker *Grey Rover* (A269, 7,500grt)./*Ambrose Greenway; Michael Lennon*

45

Left: A Russian 4,300ton Kashin class missile destroyer, in festive rather than hostile mood at Ethiopian Naval day in 1972. The Kashin is notable for being the world's first major warship class to be powered solely by gas turbines but, perhaps out of pioneering belief in safety in numbers, the propulsion machinery comprises eight gas turbine sets driving two shafts and producing 96,000shp for about 35kts. The Kashins are also powerfully armed with a variety of 3in guns, rockets, guided missiles and torpedoes./*MoD (Navy) via A. J. Watts*

Above & right: Two more pictures of Kashin class destroyers at speed in the Atlantic, showing the distinctive four large squat funnels and, in the upright shot, an interesting wake pattern. /*Both: Ambrose Greenway*

Above left & left: The Soviet's Krivaks form a follow-on class of missile destroyers to the Kashins, but with the addition of surface-to-air guided missiles that were lacking in the earlier design and thus providing a rather broader capability than the Kashins. They do it all on an appreciably smaller bulk, with a standard displacement of 3,800 tons, and they achieve a marginally better speed and an altogether neater appearance with the retained eight gas turbines all exhausting through a single big squarish uptake./*Both: MoD (Navy) via A. J. Watts*

Above: A Kresta I guided missile cruiser of the small 5,100ton class completed in the late 1960s, here pictured in the North Atlantic from a RAF Nimrod and showing an unusual square funnel casing aft of the radar tower. The class is steam turbine powered for a speed of about 33kts and is armed with four each of surface-to-surface and surface-to-air missile launchers as well as four automatic dual-purpose guns, four multi-barrel rocket launchers and 10 torpedo tubes.
/*MoD (RAF) via A. J.Watts*

Right: A Russian Krupnyi class early guided missile destroyer taking a close look at a Royal Navy Buccaneer on the *Hermes* in the Mediterranean in 1970, in the days when Soviet warships were neither so numerous nor so powerfully armed as now. The Krupnyis' mainly dual-purpose gun and torpedo armament was augmented by an early design of shipboard surface-to-surface missile and anti-submarine rockets. Some of the class were absorbed into the very similar but differently armed Kanin class.
/*MoD (Navy) via A. J. Watts*

Top left: The second class of Kresta guided missile carriers, like this one, *Admiral Isachonkov* (297, 6,000 tons) photographed from a RAF Nimrod off the Hebrides in December 1977, uses the same basic hull as the Kresta I, though it is slightly longer, but is much more powerfully armed. Armament of the Kresta IIs includes eight surface-to-surface and four surface-to-air missile launchers, 10 anti-submarine torpedo tubes and 57mm and 30mm automatic guns./*MoD (RAF) via A. J. Watts*

Left: The Polish ship *Warszawa* (275, 2,850 tons) is a SAM conversion of a Russian Kotlin-class destroyer built in the middle 1950s and transferred to Poland in 1970. The standard Kotlin was armed with guns, torpedoes and mortars and the SAM Kotlin sacrificed some of the guns for two surface-to-air missile launchers and two 12-barrel anti-submarine rocket launchers./*Stanislaro Pudlik via A. J. Watts*

Top & above: Two views of Britain's newest class of missile frigates, the Type 22, of which the first, HMS *Broadsword* (F88, 3,600 tons), is pictured here during her fitting out in 1979. The four forward Exocet and fore and after sextuple Sea Wolf missile launchers can be seen. The new class is designed as a replacement for the Leanders and is remarkable for dispensing entirely with major guns. As well as the four Exocet anti-ship missiles and two-by-six Sea Wolf anti-aircraft and anti-missile missile launchers, armament includes anti-submarine torpedo tubes and two of the new Lynx multi-role helicopters. Propulsion is by the highly efficient Tyne/Olympus gas turbine combination for economical cruising and high chase performance. /*Both: Michael Lennon*

Above: Trials of the Westland-Aérospatiale Lynx helicopter on HMS *Birmingham* (D86, c3,500 tons), the second to enter service of 10 ordered of the Type 42 Sheffield class missile destroyers. The Type 42 is another of the Royal Navy's new more-specialised classes and is designed and equipped primarily for anit-aircraft area defence. As well as the versatile Lynx helicopter and torpedo tubes, armament includes a new 4.5in automatic quick-firing gun and the new Sea Dart anti-aircraft missile system, the radars for which are housed under the domes. Gas turbine propulsion is also by the two-Tyne/two-Olympus system./*Westland Aircraft*

Below: Among the earliest of the numerous Leander class of general-purpose frigates to be launched was *Aurora* (F10, 2,450 tons), in 1964. She was also one of six of the class to be fitted to carry the Australian-designed Ikara rocket-propelled anti-submarine weapon with its homing torpedo, though in this picture, with her Wasp torpedo-armed helicopter airborne, she still carries her 4.5in guns and long-range radar aerial. All Leanders also carry the close-range Seacat anti-submarine or anti-ship missile system and Ikara Leanders also have anti-submarine mortars./*MoD, HMS Osprey*

Above: Others of the Leander class have the original twin 4.5in gun turret replaced by four of the French-designed Exocet medium-range surface-to-surface missile launchers; this picture taken in June 1977 shows HMS *Cleopatra* (F28), the first of about eight of the class so far converted. Exocet Leanders also have additional Seacat launchers fitted. Two others of the class have been fitted with the new Sea Wolf anti-missile missile system, standard on the Broadswords, for trials. */MoD, HMS Osprey*

Top: Newest warship of the Royal Netherlands Navy is the general-purpose frigate *Kortenaer* (F807, 3,500 tons), the first of a planned 12 of a 'standard' class. The class is powered by the modern Rolls-Royce Tyne/Olympus gas turbine arrangement on two shafts for a maximum speed of 30kts and will be powerfully armed with a variety of anti-aircraft and anti-ship missiles as well as a 76mm dual-purpose gun and anti-submarine torpedoes./*Netherlands Naval Shipbuilding*

Above: Pictured is the first of another new major class of the Royal Netherlands Navy, the missile frigate *Tromp* (F801, c4,000 tons), one of a pair completed in the middle 1970s to replace two pre-World War II-designed cruisers. The second ship of the class is F806 *De Ruyter,* which after completion took over the name from one of the earlier ships, which was sold to Peru and renamed *Almirante Grau* (81, 9,500 tons). The new frigates also have the Tyne/Olympus fit and are armed with Exocet, Tartar anti-aircraft and Sea Sparrow point-defence missiles, two 120mm guns and a Lynx helicopter.
/*Netherlands Naval Shipbuilding*

Top right: The missile destroyer *Rommel* (D187, 3,400 tons), one of three of the American Charles F Adams class ships built in the US for the West German Navy. The other two are D185 *Lütjens* and D186 *Mölders* and all were commissioned in the early 1970s. They are steam turbine-powered for 33kts and armament includes 5in dual-purpose guns, Tartar anti-aircraft, or Standard multi-role and Harpoon anti-submarine, missiles and torpedoes./*Mathicant via A. J. Watts*

Right: The handsome general-purpose destroyer *Småland* (J19, 2,800 tons) of the Royal Swedish Navy is one of a pair of the Halland class commissioned in the 1960s, and one of six Swedish destroyers and six frigates all due for scrapping in the near future without replacement. Swedish future policy is to rely on new fast patrol boats for short-range and submarines for longer-range operations. The two Hallands are fast ships at 35 knots and carry a big mixed armament of four 120mm guns, an early-type surface-to-surface missile launcher, two 57mm and six 40mm guns, torpedoes and up to 60 mines.
/*Royal Swedish Navy*

56

Above left: One of four of the other class of Swedish destroyers soon to be scrapped and name ship of the class, HMS *Södermanland* (J21, 2,150 tons). Also designed for a wide range of duties and a year or two younger than the Hallands, this class is powered for 34kts and backs up its retained four 120mm guns with a quadruple Seacat anti-aircraft missile launcher, four 40mm guns, a triple-barrel anti-submarine mortar, six torpedo tubes and up to 50 mines. */Royal Swedish Navy*

Left: The Royal Norwegian Navy operates five general-purpose frigates of the Oslo class, of which the *Narvik* (F304, c1,500 tons) is illustrated. The Oslo class is based on the American Dealey design, built in Norway but partly funded by the USA. The *Dealey* was a wartime design but the Norwegian ships were built in the 1960s and were modified to take modern equipment, including an octuple Sea Sparrow launcher, four Penguin anti-ship missile launchers and the Terne multiple anti-submarine system (both Penguin and Terne are Norwegian weapons) as well as torpedo tubes and four anti-aircraft guns. */ Michael Lennon*

Above: Denmark is virtually in the front line of any possible naval confrontation between the NATO and Warsaw Pact blocs and the Royal Danish Navy cooperates closely with the West German Navy in the NATO alliance. Heading the Danish Navy's offensive potential is a pair of missile frigates built in the 1960s and recently updated with new weapons, of which the *Peder Skram* (F352, c2,000 tons) is illustrated before the recent refit. The ship is powered for 30kts with diesel cruise engines and American gas turbine sprint engines and now mounts a pair of 5in and four 40mm guns, eight Harpoon surface-to-surface and octuple Sea Sparrow surface-to-air missiles and anti-ship/anti-submarine torpedoes./*Michael Lennon*

Top: Two pictures of smaller warships of navies with interests at opposite ends of the Mediterranean. Outside the Western approaches Portugal maintains a fairly numerous fleet of frigates and the one illustrated, *Almirante Magalhäes Correa* (F474, c1,500 tons), is one of three Portuguese-built versions of the US wartime Dealey class of destroyer escorts, all commissioned in the late 1960s. They are conventionally armed with 3in guns, mortars and torpedo tubes and equipped with modern sonar. Portugal also has four French-built 1,750ton Commandant Rivière class anti-submarine frigates of about similar age to the Dealeys and 10 of a joint Portuguese-Spanish 1,200ton Coutinho class, three built in Germany and the remainder in Spain, and largely fitted for anti-submarine work./*Inter-Air Press*

Above: At the eastern end Turkey straddles the gateway to the Black Sea and maintains about a dozen ships of destroyer/ frigate size, mainly conversions of American World War II or early postwar designs. An exception is the two-ship frigate class of which the *Berk* (D358, 1,450 tons) is illustrated wearing her finery for the 1977 Royal Review at Spithead. The two ships, commissioned in the middle 1970s, carry four 3in guns and anti-submarine torpedoes and are the first major warships built in Turkey./*Michael Lennon*

In the middle Mediterranean the Italian Navy maintains roundly two dozen warships from frigate up to light cruiser designation, two of the latest of which are illustrated here.

Top: The *Lupo* (F564, 2,300 tons) is lead ship of a class of four general-purpose frigates completed between 1977 and 1979. They have gas turbine/diesel propulsion for top speeds of 34 or 22kts and are armed with a 127mm dual-purpose gun, one octal Sea Sparrow point defence and eight Otomat surface-surface missile launchers, two triple anti-submarine launchers and a helicopter./*Italian Navy*

Above: The *Ardito* (D550, 3,600 tons) is one of a pair of guided-missile destroyers completed in 1972-73 with all-gas turbine machinery to provide for 33kts. Armament includes a Standard surface-air missile launcher, two 127mm and four 76mm guns, six anti-submarine and four dual-purpose torpedo tubes and two helicopters./*Italian Navy*

Above: The French Navy is the fourth in the world size and power, after the US, the USSR and the UK. French warships occasionally exercise with those of NATO navies but most are deployed in the currently uncertain Mediterranean and the remainder are spread rather thinly on the French Atlantic coastline and to cover her remaining widespread commitments. The *Duguay-Trouin* (D611, 4,800 tons) is one of the three-ship Tourville class of missile destroyers completed in the middle 1970s. They are steam turbine-powered for 31kts and initially armed with three 100mm dual-purpose guns, two triple Exocet launchers, a Malafon rocket/torpedo launcher, two anti-submarine torpedo tubes and two Lynx helicopters. The third of the class, *De Grasse* (D612) had a Crotale surface-to-air missile launcher in place of the third gun mounted amidships above the hangar and this picture shows that *Duguay-Trouin* has also lost the after gun./*Michael Lennon*

Below: Two earlier and rather faster and bigger guided-missile destroyers were the Suffren class, of which the second, *Duquesne* (D603, 5,000 tons) is shown. With their enormous radomes identification of the Suffrens should not be a problem (although the Dutch Tromps' are nearly as big). They have the comparatively high top speed of 34kts from steam turbine machinery and are well armed for a mixed role with two 100mm and two 30mm guns, a twin Masurca anti-aircraft missile launcher – well in evidence in the picture, with the two directors above and ahead – a Malafon launcher and torpedo tubes. / *Michael Lennon*

Above: The *Aconit* (D609, 3,450 tons) is a one-off anti-submarine frigate, originally classed as a corvette, with a rather lower than normal fleet speed of 27kts, commissioned in 1973. General armament includes single dual-purpose 100mm guns fore and aft and four Exocet surface-to-surface missile launchers, and anti-submarine weapons are a Malafon rocket/torpedo launcher, a quadruple mortar and two torpedo tubes. The *Aconit* was in fact used to test and work up several new weapons and systems and was the first to be equipped with the French SENIT tactical information system./*Michael Lennon*

Below: The anti-submarine frigate *Udaygiri* (F34, c2,500 tons) represents India's small but growing fleet of modern ships, now being built in Indian yards to the British Leander design. They are to support the country's elderly single aircraft carrier, two light cruisers and about a dozen mixed earlier British frigates. The Indian Leanders so far completed are armed with Seacat anti-aircraft missile launchers and various anti-submarine weapons and each carries a French Alouette helicopter. /*Michael Lennon*

Top: The Japanese Navy, or Maritime Defence Force as it is officially named, has a fairly strong fleet of destroyers, frigates and fast patrol craft. A growing proportion of the vessels are modern, fast and missile-armed, though some date from the 1950s, when postwar restrictions on the building of warships in Japan were lifted. Pictured here during a courtesy visit to Portsmouth in August 1979 is anti-submarine destroyer *Mochizuki* (DD166, 3,100 tons), one of a class of four completed in the late 1960s, steam powered for 32kts, armed with dual-purpose 5in guns, anti-submarine torpedoes and ASROC launchers and carrying a helicopter./*Michael Lennon*

Above: The *Brisbane* (41, 3,400 tons) is one of three US Adams-class missile destroyers operated by the Royal Australian Navy, to support its recently acquired Perry-class patrol frigates (more of which are building) and a fleet of elderly Daring-class destroyers and modernised River-class anti-submarine frigates. The *Brisbane* and her two sisters are powered for 33kts and carry two 5in dual-purpose guns, torpedo tubes and a variety of anti-surface and anti-aircraft missiles./*Michael Lennon*

Top: One of the Royal Canadian Navy's largish fleet of anti-submarine destroyers, the *Annapolis* (265, 2,450 tons). The ships are in three groups variously armed for anti-submarine work, *Annapolis* and a sister ship *Nipigon* (266) having two 3in guns, a triple mortar, variable-depth sonar and a helicopter. / *Michael Lennon*

Above: Brazil now has the most modern navy in South America, brought right up to date with the six Vosper Thornycroft Mark

10 frigates, delivery of which has just been completed; four were built in the UK Vosper Thornycroft yards and two in Brazil with the company's technical assistance. The group comprises four anti-submarine and two general-purpose ships, the one illustrated, *Liberal* (F43, 3,200 tons) being of the former type. They are all Olympus gas turbine/diesel powered for 31kts and carry a Lynx helicopter, the anti-submarine versions being additionally armed with 4.5in and 40mm guns, one Ikara anti-ship and two triple Seacat anti-aircraft missile launchers, rocket launchers and torpedo tubes./*Vosper Thornycroft Ltd*

Above & top right: Two views of USS *Virginia* (CGN38, 10,000 tons dl), name ship of the US Navy's latest class of nuclear-powered guided-missile frigates, designed as escorts for the nuclear carrier-headed battle groups. The ships are very big for the escort frigate role, providing a spacious layout for a generous armament without the crowding evident, for example, in Russian ships, and excellent crew quarters. Weapons include two twin launchers that will take anti-submarine or anti-aircraft missiles, two dual-purpose automatic 5in guns, two aimable triple torpedo tubes and a helicopter housed in an underdeck hangar. The square on the foredeck is the mark for helicopter provisioning./*Both: US Navy*

Right: A view of the *Virginia*'s afterdeck showing the multi-purpose missile launcher and automatic 5in gun and one of the torpedo launchers on the left of the picture. As well as current Standard anti-aircraft and ASROC anti-submarine missiles, the Mark 26 launcher is also expected to handle the new Harpoon anti-ship missile./*US Navy*

Top left: One of four remaining 1959-60 conversions of wartime Cleveland class light cruisers to carry guided missiles, USS *Little Rock* (CG64, 10,700 tons), here pictured firing Talos surface-to-air missiles. As well as a twin Talos launcher, the *Little Rock* is armed with three 6in and two 5in guns./*US Navy*

Left: USS *Spruance* (DD963, 8,000 tons dl), lead ship of a class of 30 missile destroyers, pictured during her shakedown cruise in November 1975. The Spruance class is the first major US warship to be powered by gas turbines only, for 31kts, and armament includes ASROC and Mark 26 or Sea Sparrow launchers, two 5in dual-purpose guns, two triple torpedo tubes and one large or two small helicopters./*US Navy*

Top: Another of the US Navy's nuclear-powered missile frigates, *South Carolina* (CGN37, 10,200 tons dl), one of a pair that immediately preceded the Virginia class and established the pattern for their design. Armament includes an ASROC 8-tube and two single Tartar surface-to-air launchers, two 5in dual-purpose guns, four torpedo tubes and two helicopters. /*Inter-Air Press*

Above: USS *Oliver Hazard Perry* (FFG7, c3,500 tons dl), the first of an intended big class of missile frigates, is pictured here in February 1978 just after completion. The class is gas turbine powered for 29kts and carries a dual-purpose Standard/Harpoon launcher, a 76mm dual-purpose gun, a Vulcan-Phalanx 20mm close-in weapon system and two light helicopters. /*US Navy*

Assault Craft and Minor Warships

Below: Three of the US Navy's assault ships on an amphibious forces exercise with the Sixth Fleet in the Mediterranean. Left to right: A tank landing ship (LST) of the 20-strong Newport class; an amphibious transport dock (LPD) of the 10,000ton Austin class; and a dock landing ship, LSD34 *Hermitage* of the 6,900ton Thomaston class./*Ambrose Greenway*

Bottom & right: Two pictures of the tank landing ship USS *Spartanburg Country* (LST1192), demonstrating the opening of her bow doors and lowering the ramp, during a NATO exercise. / *Both: US Navy*

Left & below: Two views of the huge amphibious assault ships of the recently commissioned Tarawa class, LHA1 *Tarawa* herself and LHA2 *Saipan*. The new five-ship class has been designed to combine the roles of two types – transport and assault ship – while at the same time providing more cargo capacity. It has a deep-load displacement of 40,000 tons, is 820ft long and over 100ft wide and unaided can carry and embark/disembark 2,000 troops and their equipment, as well as up to 32 helicopters or V/STOL aircraft. It is powered for 25kts and is armed with dual-purpose guns and anti-aircraft missiles and some of its aircraft could be equipped for defence. /*Both: US Navy*

Right: An overall view of the class of ship in the middle of the picture on page 68, the amphibious transport dock LPD7 *Cleveland.* The 10,000ton ship is powered for 20kts and is armed with eight anti-aircraft guns and possibly some of its complement of six heavy stores helicopters could be armed. There is accommodation for 900 troops and all their equipment, side doors in the hull provide for roll-on/roll-off, a variety of landing craft is carried and the big flightdeck allows for a rapid stores handling by the ship's own and other ships' helicopters. / *US Navy*

Below right: An air-cushion amphibious assault landing craft (AALC) under test by the US Navy. The 170ton vehicle is powered by gas turbines driving eight centrifugal fans and can carry up to 60 tons of cargo at around 50kts over land or water. / *US Navy*

Top: One of a pair of French Navy 5,700ton ships (dock), L9021 *Ouragan*. The ships are diesel powered for about 17 knots and are armed with six 30mm anti-aircraft guns and two 120mm mortars and there is a small helicopter deck. Up to 500 troops can be carried over short distances and two large tank landing craft (LCTs) or up to 18 small landing craft (LCMs) can be handled by ship's crane or floated into the stern dock. */A. J. Watts*

Above: One of a pair of Royal Navy Fearless-class c12,000ton landing ships (dock), L11 *Intrepid*. Geared steam turbines provide up to 21kts and weapons include quadruple Seacat anti-aircraft missile launchers and two 40mm AA guns. Up to six

Wessex helicopters are carried, there is a docking well at the stern served by four 100ton capacity LCMs and four 43ft landing craft are carried in davits. Each ship can carry up to 700 troops and all their equipment and is equipped with communications and services for headquarters duties. */Michael Lennon*

Right: The other ship of the British pair, HMS *Fearless* (L10), in the Mediterranean, with the Type 12 Rothesay-class anti-submarine frigate *Lowestoft* (F103, 2,400 tons) coming alongside to refuel. One of the LSD's landing craft, which can carry 35 equipped troops or two light vehicles, can be seen in davits. */Ambrose Greenway*

Left & below: Two landing craft built by Brooke Marine, a company that produces a variety of fast patrol and specialised craft. Below is a 1,650ton 10kt logistics vessel for the British Ministry of Defence that can carry and beach-land through bow doors up to 350 tons of mixed cargo or five main battle tanks. Left is a 2,000ton 12kt landing support ship for the Sultanate of Oman. It can carry about 200 troops and 550 tons of mixed stores or eight main battle tanks. It is armed with an Oto-Melara 76/62 gun and has helicopter landing and fuelling facilities. / *Brooke Marine Ltd*

Right: Three mine countermeasures vessels of the permanent NATO Standing Naval Force Channel (STANAVFORCHAN) set up in 1973 and until recently formed from about a dozen ships provided by the Belgian, British, Danish, Dutch and German navies. In 1979 the United States Navy added two of its minesweepers to the force./*NATO*

Below right: The modern Danish minelayer *Moen* (N82, 2,000 tons), one of a class of four. They and two later ships play a large part in the defence of the Danish Straits. Each ship is armed with 3in guns and is to be fitted with Sea Sparrow missiles and can lay 400 mines with high precision aided by electronic equipment./*Michael Lennon*

Top left: The *Cybèle* (M712, 490 tons) is one of a class of five French minehunters with a speed of 15kts, or 7kts when sweeping. They are fitted with modern detection equipment and armed with a 20mm cannon and two remotely controlled minesweeping vehicles./*Michael Lennon*

Left: Sweden sets considerable store on mine warfare and equips most of her warships to lay mines of various types. Impending scrapping of her destroyers and frigates is partly offset by the commissioning of two new minelayers, of which the *Visborg* (MO3, 2,550 tons), is illustrated, although they and a third similar vessel planned also serve as submarine depot ships and are on the big and slow side for best minelaying efficiency./*Royal Swedish Navy via A. J. Watts*

Top: The Swedish Navy is not very well equipped for minesweeping and a project to build minehunters has not materialised. Illustrated is HMS *Arkö* (M57, 285 tons) one of 12 coastal minesweepers completed between 1958 and 1964. /*Royal Swedish Navy via A. J. Watts*

Above: The Belgian minesweeper *Breydel* (M906, 720 tons) one of seven US M50 Type 504 ships transferred to the Belgian Navy./*Michael Lennon*

Above: Two Royal Norwegian Navy Storm class fast patrol boats, *Hvass* (P972, 150 tons) leading, escorting some of the 'Tall Ships', including *Kruzenshtern, Christian Radich* and *Dar Pomorza*, into *Oslo.* Storm-class and derivative Hauk class boats have a speed well over 30kts and are armed with Penguin surface-to-surface missiles and guns and/or torpedoes.
/ *Ambrose Greenway*

Top right & centre right: With the scrapping of her bigger warships Sweden will rely heavily on her fast well-armed FPB, two types of which are illustrated. P151 *Jägaren* is the prototype of the latest Hugin class based on the Norwegian Storm design, of which a further 16 boats are in course of delivery. They are classed as coastal patrol boats and armed

with a Bofors 57mm gun and six Penguin missile launchers. T124 *Castor* is a long-range fast attack boat of the Spica 1 class armed with a 57mm Bofors gun and six 21in torpedoes. Both types have modern communication and fire-control equipment.
/ *Both: Royal Swedish Navy via A. J. Watts*

Right: The Royal Danish Navy's fast patrol boat *Willemoes* (P549,260 tons) is lead-boat of a 10-strong class built in the 1970s and powered by Rolls-Royce Proteus gas turbines for a speed of 40kts. They are armed with a 76mm Oto-Melara gun, Harpoon surface-to-surface missiles and torpedoes and are equipped to lay mines, stores of which can be seen lining the deck in the picture./*Royal Danish Navy via A. J. Watts*

Top: P637 *L'Etourdi* is one of a class of 14 320ton 19kt coastal escorts of the French Navy. They carry two 40mm anti-aircraft guns and a variety of anti-surface mortars./*Michael Lennon*

Above: HMS *Orkney* (P299, 1,250 tons) is one of the Royal Navy's new Islands class of five offshore patrol craft designed specifically for the more-distant work involved in fishery and oilfield protection. They represent the first purpose-built ships for the role and are equipped to work as part of an integrated air and sea protection network. Two further Island class ships are under construction./*Michael Lennon*

Top right: One of the Royal Navy's BH7 55ton combat amphibious craft by British Hovercraft Corporation, designed to take a variety of surface-to-surface and anti-aircraft missiles and guns. The craft can take up to five crew and a 7ton weapon load at speeds up to 60kts, with a range up to 10 hours. /*British Hovercraft Corp*

Right: Artist's impression of the Boeing Jetfoil due for delivery to the Royal Navy in late 1979 and to be named HMS *Speedy*. The craft is a development of the Boeing commercial hydrofoil, which is in widespread passenger service, and will be used to evaluate the craft in fishery and oilfield protection work. As well as the gas turbine/waterjet propulsion system giving a foilborne speed of 43kts, the *Speedy* has conventional diesel power to provide also long hullborne cruising range. /*Boeing Marine Systems*

Left: As well as ships of frigate/destroyer size, Vosper Thornycroft designs and builds craft for offshore and coastal patrol work from corvettes down to 60ft patrol boats. Examples built for various navies are illustrated, top to bottom: P206, *Menzel Bourguiba*, one of two 130ft patrol craft for Tunisia armed with two 40mm guns *(Vosper Thornycroft); Erin' Mi* (F83,750 tons), one of two 27kt Mark 9 corvettes with modern guns and missiles for Nigeria, which already operates two VT Mark 3 corvettes *(Michael Lennon);* and P15 *Patria,* one of six 37m 30kt patrol boats armed with a 40mm gun and guided missiles for Venezuela *(Vosper Thornycroft).*

Top: The Japanese patrol boat *Shikine* (PM21, 465 tons) is one of five Chifuri class boats completed in the early 1950s. Diesels provide 16kts and a 3in gun can be carried. The boats are also used on hydrographic and navigational aids duties.
/Via A. J. Watts

Above: One of the potent Israeli Reshef class patrol boats of which 12 have so far been completed, including six for South Africa built three in Israel and three in Durban. They displace 415 tons and are diesel powered for 32kts and have very long range. Armament comprises six Gabriel or four Harpoon (when available) missiles and two 76mm OTO-Melara guns.
/Michael Lennon

Top left: Halter Marine Inc designs and builds a variety of fast patrol craft for navies and coastguards. The vessel illustrated is an example of the Halmar Broadsword, a 105ft class built for some Central and South American navies which can be variously armed and powered for speeds up to 40kts. */Halter Marine Inc.*

Left: The United States Navy has been experimenting with the use of hydrofoil and air-cushion craft in fast patrol work for several years. The hydrofoil research ship *Plainview* (AGEHI) leading the hydrofoil patrol craft *High Point* (PCH1) at high speed on foils./*US Navy*

Above: The *Sparviero* (P420, 62 tons) is the first of a class of hydrofoils designed in Italy as a substitute for the much bigger US 'NATO' Pegasus class after Italy and West Germany dropped out of the Pegasus arrangement on the ground of steeply rising cost. The *Sparviero* has a 4,500hp waterjet unit to give up to 50kts on the foils and a diesel/propeller set for hull-borne cruising. Armament consists of one OTO-Melara 76mm gun and two Otomat missiles./*Italian Navy*

Left & top: Two views of a Boeing hydrofoil missile-firing patrol craft at speed on foils and firing one of its missiles. After trials, one of the Boeing craft entered service with the USN in 1977 as USS *Pegasus* (PHMI). The Boeing 240ton craft is powered by General Electric gas turbine for 40kts and 600 miles range on the hull. In both cases propulsion is by Aerojet water jets. */Both: Boeing Marine Systems*

Above: One of two surface-effect craft in experimental service with the USN, SES 100B, by Bell Aerospace at a speed in excess of 70kts in the Gulf of Mexico./*US Navy*

Auxiliaries

Below: Underway replenishment demonstrated by the US Navy in the Mediterranean; the missile cruiser *Albany* (CG10, 13,900 tons) and Knox class anti-submarine frigate *W. S. Sims* (FF1059, 3,000 tons) flank store ship USNS *Rigel* while the fast store ship *Sylvania* (AFS2) serves Adams class missile destroyer *Richard E. Byrd* (DDG 23, 3,400 tons) astern./*US Navy*

Bottom: Replenishment event during a NATO exercise, with American fleet oiler *Neosho* (AO143) flanked by British County class missile destroyer *Hampshire* (D06, 5,450 tons) and landing ship dock *Fearless* (L10, 11,100 tons). /*Ambrose Greenway*

Right: A full view of USS *Neosho*, with the *Hampshire* beyond, as HMS *Fearless* drops astern./*Ambrose Greenway*

Bottom right: Replenishment in the Pacific during Exercise Maflex-78, as a Boeing-Vertol CH-46 Sea Knight from combat store ship USS *San Jose* (AFS7) carries a netload of supplies to amphibious command ship USS *Blue Ridge* (LCC 19, 19,300 tons dl)./*US Navy*

A sequence of pictures showing one of the hazards of underway replenishment as oiler and recipient throw up a fountain of spray as they collide, and end up with a parted hose. /Ambrose Greenway, Popperfoto

Above right: Two British ships in a part of the world where such mishaps might very well occur, though conditions look quiet enough in the picture. The Royal Fleet Auxiliary (RFA), fleet tanker Olwen (A122, 18,600grt), and HMS Hampshire off Cape Forward in the Magellan Strait./Ambrose Greenway

Right: The anti-submarine/commando carrier Bulwark (R08) approaching the fleet tanker RFA Olmeda, sister ship of the Olwen, to refuel, with Type 61 aircraft-direction frigate HMS Chichester (F59, 2,200 tons) alongside./Ambrose Greenway

Top: That the Mediterranean can provide distinctly unfriendly conditions is illustrated by this picture of the British fleet replenishment ship *Regent* (A486, 18,000grt) ploughing into a heavy sea during a NATO exercise./*Ambrose Greenway*

Above: Just how much of the *Regent* had gone submarine is indicated by this picture of sister ship RFA *Resource* (A480) moored in a quiet sea./*Michael Lennon*

Right: American amphibious cargo ship and British fleet replenishment ship keep company, with Gearing-class anti-submarine destroyer *Basilone* (DD824, 2,450 tons) in attendance, during a NATO exercise in the Mediterranean. / *Ambrose Greenway*

Top left & left: Pictures showing two aspects of the latest British RFAs, the 9,800grt afloat support ships A385 *Fort Grange* and A386 *Fort Austin*. Each ship will operate a naval helicopter to provide the RFAs with anti-submarine protection, as demonstrated by the No824 Squadron Sea King about to land on one of the two helicopter spots on *Fort Grange*.
/Michael Lennon; MoD, HMS Excellent

Top: The Royal Navy's Hovercraft Trials Unit carries out evaluation and development of several types of hovercraft in various roles, including patrol and mine countermeasures duties. Here a BHC SRN6 craft is pictured when it provided support for a Royal Marines detachment in the Falkland Islands.
/British Hovercraft Corp

Above: The French logistic support ship *Loire* (A615, 2,250 tons, 15kts), one of five basically similar fleet auxiliaries each fitted for a particular specialist purpose. The *Loire* serves as a minesweeper base ship and is armed with three 40mm anti-aircraft guns and carries a helicopter./*Michael Lennon*

Top: The *Gustav Zédé* (759, 800 tons), named appropriately after the French submarine pioneer, is used by the French Navy for underwater experimental and trials work. The ship is one of a class of German aircraft tenders, originally named *Greif* and built at Stettin in 1937./*Michael Lennon*

Above: The Italian fleet replenishment tanker *Stromboli* (A5327, 8,700 tons dl) was completed in 1975 and was joined by sister ship *Vesuvio* in 1978. The class can carry three grades of oil as well as dry stores and has a helicopter pad but does not carry a helicopter. Diesel power on a single shaft provides up to 20 knots and armament comprises one 76mm and two 40mm guns./*Italian Navy*